Malcolm
Rivkin
245 Fairmount Ave
Hyde Park
Mass.

NATALIE MAISIE

AND

PAVILASTUKAY

ALSO BY JOHN MASEFIELD

PLAYS:

THE FAITHFUL: *A Tragedy in Three Acts*
GOOD FRIDAY: *A Play in Verse*
ESTHER. (*Adapted and partially translated from the French of Jean Racine*)
BERENICE. (*Adapted from the French of Jean Racine*)
MELLONEY HOLTSPUR; or, The Pangs of Love. *A Play in Four Acts*
A KING'S DAUGHTER: *A Tragedy in Verse in Four Acts*
THE TRIAL OF JESUS
THE TRAGEDY OF NAN
TRISTAN AND ISOLT: *A Play in Verse*
THE COMING OF CHRIST
EASTER: *A Play for Singers*
END AND BEGINNING

POETRY:

DAUBER
THE DAFFODIL FIELDS
PHILIP THE KING AND OTHER POEMS
LOLLINGDON DOWNS AND OTHER POEMS, WITH SONNETS
A POEM AND TWO PLAYS. (*Rosas, a poem; The Locked Chest; The Sweeps of Ninety-Eight*)
REYNARD THE FOX
ENSLAVED AND OTHER POEMS
RIGHT ROYAL
SELECTED POEMS
KING COLE AND OTHER POEMS
COLLECTED POEMS
MIDSUMMER NIGHT AND OTHER TALES IN VERSE
MINNIE MAYLOW'S STORY AND OTHER TALES AND SCENES
A TALE OF TROY
A LETTER FROM PONTUS AND OTHER VERSE
SOME VERSES TO SOME GERMANS
GAUTAMA THE ENLIGHTENED

FICTION:

SARD HARKER
ODTAA
THE MIDNIGHT FOLK
THE HAWBUCKS
THE BIRD OF DAWNING
THE TAKING OF THE GRY
THE BOX OF DELIGHTS
VICTORIOUS TROY
EGGS AND BAKER
THE SQUARE PEG
DEAD NED
LIVE AND KICKING NED
BASILISSA
CONQUER

GENERAL:

GALLIPOLI
THE OLD FRONT LINE
ST. GEORGE AND THE DRAGON
THE BATTLE OF THE SOMME
RECENT PROSE
WITH THE LIVING VOICE
THE WANDERER OF LIVERPOOL
POETRY: A Lecture
THE CONWAY
THE NINE DAYS WONDER
IN THE MILL

NATALIE MAISIE

AND

PAVILASTUKAY

TWO TALES IN VERSE

BY

JOHN MASEFIELD

NEW YORK

THE MACMILLAN COMPANY

1942

Set up and electrotyped. Published June, 1942.

FIRST PRINTING.

PRINTED IN THE UNITED STATES OF AMERICA
AMERICAN BOOK–STRATFORD PRESS, INC., NEW YORK

To

My Wife

NATALIE MAISIE

AND

PAVILASTUKAY

NATALIE MAISIE

A Tale of the Emperor Peter the Great of Russia

The deed described in this tale, the hiding of a girl by her foster-parents from the pursuit of the Czar, is said to have happened during the early eighteenth century.

Russian familiar names have often several forms: Marfa, Marfenka, Marfoutka, Marfoushka; Natalie, Natasha, Nasha; Olga, Olushka; Prokhor, Proshka, Proushka.

PROLOGUE

Ere the Czar Peter, that tempestuous Prince,
Wore Russia's crown, eight generations since,
An English merchant, settled there for trade,
Married a dark-haired, lovely Russian maid.

One only child, a girl, this lady bare;
A wood-wife was her foster-mother there.
The child grew into girlhood with the grace
Of a glad blush upon a darling face.

Now all the tumult of the blazing star
That brightened and made beautiful the Czar,
Burned into purpose of a town to be
Queen in the North, triumphant on the sea.
St. Petersburg, the new, ship-splendid town
Stood at his urge, the jewel of his crown.

Thither our merchant and his household came.

Natalie Maisie was his daughter's name.
A lovely girl as gentle and as gay
As hawthorn blossom in a sunny May
Dark-eyed, dark-haired, and never to be seen
By any man but longed to call her queen.

There Michael, a young sailor, won her heart.

His Fleet awaited order to depart
Upon a cruise, but ere the signal flew,
Imperial heralds went the City through
Bidding all rank and office, great and least,
To the Czar's Palace, to a farewell Feast.

Time, ever-passing, brought that night of nights.
Palacewards blazed the thousand carriage lights,
Mortals out-glittering gold and silver pheasants,
Passed up the scarlet stairways to the Presence,
Or Presence Chamber, where a voice of brass
Roared a mismade announce of who each was.
Those coming up beheld the shining swarms,
Jewels and feathers, swords and uniforms,
And heard the hundreds shouting to be heard
While in the tuning band the 'cellos burred.
Then, to a bugle-call, came heralds' cries
"Russians, prepare to greet Their Majesties."
Instantly, then, all surged to enter-in
The swelter and the glitter and the din.

Natalie Maisie entered to the glare
That lit her dream, her first Imperial Ball,
A thousand candles shone in sconces there,
A thousand weapons gleamed upon the wall.
Michael, her sailor-lover, gave a call
And hurried to her, saying "You were right.
We sail upon the midnight tide to-night.

We are all here, we sailors of the Fleet,
And though to part from you is bitter pain
It is great honour to be reckoned meet
To bring our Navy to the Spanish Main.
And from the Service view, it is a gain,
For all we seamen of the Western Ocean
On our return, are certain of promotion.

We have till midnight still, and then, the Czar
Will wish us fortune and away we steer.
Courage, although Campeachy may seem far,
I shall be back beside you in a year.
I had a happy omen coming here . . .
Down by the Docks, some Forest people stood
With timber-waggons from the Outer Wood . . ."

"You mean, my darling foster-kin?" said she.
"Yes . . . Prokhor, from the forest, with his mate,
Come, with their daughter to take note of me
(Being your lover), body, voice and gait.
They said 'Miss Natalie is an estate
Richer than any crown,' and much they grieve
They cannot speak with you before they leave.

They must be starting for the woods to-night.
They are good, simple souls, adoring you."
"O, I would love to see them if I might,
The faithfullest dear souls, Earth ever knew.
My foster-sister, Olga, with them, too.
I'm glad you've seen them; would that I might see.
Might we not catch them? Will you come with me?"

"They may have started, and, alas, my Sweet,
My orders are to bide in presence here
Until the Czar has spoken to the Fleet.
And Gold-Stick yonder orders us to clear.
Now, since we must be parted for a year
Let us enjoy the dance and mock at fates.
See, the band tuned, and the conductor waits."

They smiled upon her parents, and away
Into the dance the two young lovers sped,
Snatching delight to keep despair at bay,
Dancing, to heed not how the minutes fled.
Tiny white flowers coronied her head,
White was her frock with one small crimson rose.
No other dancers there compared with those.

The courtiers watched them, wondering to see
The bright-eyed grace and beauty of the pair
Fresh from some faery kingdom, he and she,
Rapt in the dance, forgetting their despair,
Away, away, they floated upon air
Perfectly matched, the ball-room's queen and king
The dancers stayed, to watch so fair a thing.

The two alone held the great gleaming space
The other couples gathered to the wall,
And beauty came upon each watching face
Seeing life timed thus to the music's fall.
The drummers thundered the Imperial Call.
Silent were Polish flute and violin.
Czar Peter led the Empress Catherine in.

Like ship and compass were that startling two;
Action heroic and direction wise;
He, braced and driving with the urge to do;
She, ever pointing his rude enterprise;
He had a wolf's mouth and a wild bear's eyes,
And shipwright's hands, and she, an oval face,
Dark, exquisite brown hair and dancer's grace.

Michael and Natalie sped from the floor.
One said "The Emperor watched you all this while,
He and the Empress, standing at the door."
The Imperial couple passing down the aisle
Stopped, as they neared; Czar Peter with a smile
Turning to Natalie, said, "Maiden . . . see . . .
Whose dainty little daughter may you be?"

Curtseying, scared, yet in intense delight,
Blushing and looking at her very best,
Her maiden soul in all its merry might
Replied to him; he answered with a jest.
"I'll be your partner later; meanwhile . . . rest . . .
And this young man's a sailor, outward bound . . .
Young sir; respects . . . a pretty girl you've found."

So, smiling, nodding through the crowd he swept,
Cheered, and saluted by the trumpet blast
His ushers backed before him as he stept
The women sank in curtseys as he passed.
One little warning glance the Empress cast
On Natalie, and then the royal pair
Climbed the great scarlet dais and throned them there.

Natalie's heart leaped, for she stood among
The loveliest women of her time and race,
The very roses of the Russian young,
And he, the Czar, had praised her to her face.
Yet like a doe deer with a wolf in chase
She trembled at the Empress' warning glance.
Again the music called her to the dance.

When the dance ended, maids in white and blue
Decked the vast room with tables and with trays
Glasses and wine, and now the lovers knew
The moment near for parting of the ways.
The silver trumpets shrilled into a praise.
The Czar moved slowly to the platform edge.
And cried "My Russians . . . I've a health to pledge.

Among you stand the Future of Our Fleet,
The Service We with Our own hands began.
The squadron and the convoy lie complete.
Weapons, equipment, gear, for ship and man.
Their purpose is a portion of a plan
We make for Russia, whom Our strength and strife
Shall always serve, as long as We have life.

Who had imagined, twenty years ago
That City, port and squadron would be here?
The will for splendid Russia makes her so;
All lands are splendid, if men hold them dear.
Greece was but mountain, marshes and a mere
But every Art and Science lightening Earth
Quickened in Greece and came to glorious birth,

And spread across the world to every land,
Except to Russia, she alone lay rude
Uncouth in spirit, clumsy in the hand,
Like to her bears, a shaggy, savage brood.
Her nobles merely huntsmen and as crude,
Her people, boors; all, swinish in the sty.
We said 'We will bring Russia light or die.'

So off We went to work, to learn Our parts
To make this Russia splendid on the sea.
We sent our youth abroad to learn the arts,
To forget sport and learn civility;
To send the mind wherever Thought may be
To gladden man or glorify his day,
And build an Athens in this northern clay.

My Russians, a beginning has been made.
To-night, our Navy with its convoy starts
A Tropic, Mexic and Campeachy Trade,
To carry Russian goods to western marts;
To bring us commerce precious in the arts,
As dyewoods for fine scarlets, indigoes,
And cochineals and madders, blue to rose.

Moreover, they will bring the woods of price,
Slow-growing tropic timber, trebly hard,
That polish into surfaces like ice,
Or fashion gun-decks in the Navy Yard,
And pines with which our squadrons may be sparred,
Squarer and stronger than the Swedish pine;
And dust of gold, a foreign wealth, in fine.

Now, fill your glasses, Russians, drink with me
Success to all our sailors as they go:
Triumph, and safe return from over sea
With Russia greater than the land we know.
Russia must triumph over every foe,
Now, Russian sailors, overcome or die.
Your health . . . three cheers . . . one more . . . and now Good-bye."

It was Good-bye, and crueller to bear
Than aught that Natalie and Michael knew,
One little blinding instant, then despair;
The Naval officers together drew.
The Czar raised cheers, the boatswains' whistles blew:
The drums receded with feet marching on,
And Natalie was there, with Michael gone.

But as a woman can, she hid her woe
Before the courtiers; and away, away,
Attendants scattered powdered chalk like snow
And rushed the wine and tables to a bay,
The cimbals clashed, the band began to play
The couples danced, and suddenly the Czar
Was at her elbow, saying "Here we are.

Now dance with me, Miss Natalie, the belle."
His strong arm plucked her out into the rush
And Maisie knew he danced supremely well:
With perfect skill he twirled her through the crush,
And she, now white with terror, red with blush,
Lost with despair for Michael gone, took heart
At dancing with her equal in the art.

She could observe him when her partner set;
A compact, driving force on living springs,
With Tartar eyes, most savage, black as jet,
And hands all tarry-brown, unlike a King's.
The muscle and the fire of his flings
Were like a colt's, his face was pale and fierce,
And when he smiled, its purpose seemed to pierce.

He wore an English costume, blue and white,
The buttons gleamed with facets of cut steel,
It seemed disguise on so much greed of might,
Such will to bring the stubborn bear to heel.
"A will to do, and not a nerve to feel,"
She told herself, and trembled at the thought
"The Czar has picked me out of all the Court."

It was a triumph but it terrified.
And when, after the dance, she heard him say
"I'm for the throne, now; come and sit beside,"
She quaked, but had no bolt-hole but obey.
She saw that every eye was turned her way
She sat upon the gilt step of the throne
Above the room, the Czar and she alone.

"Listen, my sweet Natasha," said the Czar,
"My light-foot gay gazelle and dainty deer,
Your beauty both deserves and needs a star,
Lieutenant, bring that tray of jewels here.
This shining spray will make you without peer.
Girl, put this jewel in her lovely hair."
A Maid of Honour came and set it there,

And held a glass for Natalie to see
The frosty star upon her beauty set
Twined in a silver ivy filigree
Part bridal wreath, and partly coronet.
"There," said the Czar, "you will not soon forget
Your first Imperial Ball, nor I, I think.
Now, little angel, shall we dance or drink?"

All this was public as the Market Square
High on the dais, watched by every eye,
And even ladies common as the air
Assumed a chastity from jealousy.
"Nashy, you're tempting as a birthday pie,"
He cried, "I'll bite you, if I find a chance.
Now answer, darling, shall we drink or dance?"

Trembling, and horrified and terrified,
Ashamed and knowing not what way to take
"Dance, if it please you, Sire," she replied.
"Dance . . . that's the answer all you women make.
Dance . . . in a ball-room hot enough to bake.
Strike up Tziganes; if you had been a boy,
You'd have said 'Drink' for drink's my Russia's joy."

It had been his, and lately, as she knew
Whenas he dragged her to the dancing-floor
And hugged her as he twirled the measure through.
No pretty girl could loathe a partner more.
He stamped upon the beat, he sang, he swore,
He bade the band play quicker with more noise,
But danced light as a feather and with poise.

"Life, girl, you dance," he cried, "our steps agree.
We Russians are the dancers of the earth.
England and Holland triumph on the sea;
And France excels in manners and in mirth.
Spain's for austerity and pride and dearth,
But all who cherish order above prancing
Know, Holy Russia is supreme for dancing."

The dancers left the floor to watch the pair,
"His Majesty's enamoured," they exclaimed.
"Look at him with the little baggage there."
The ladies said "She ought to be ashamed."
The men remarked "Our town-bull is untamed . . .
And she's as fresh as any cherry-flower.
Another private palace and a dower."

Some insolent Court-ladies, rouged and masked
Scenting the scandal watched with jealous eyes.
"His mistress, or his natural child?" they asked.
"A school-girl, with the Catechism prize."
But Peter, hot upon his enterprise,
Danced with his partner off the dancing-floor
Into the quiet of a corridor

"Nashy, you're beautiful enough to eat,"
The Czar exclaimed, "And dance like thistle-down,
Joy in the soul and fire in the feet,
And hair my special passion of dark brown.
See here, some little trinkets for your gown . . ."
He led into a room of precious things
Offered to Russia by this planet's kings.

He gave a watch, a miracle of art,
Fashioned in Paris for the Empress' wrist;
And Spanish-Indian rings that twined apart
Or clasped the wearer at a finger-twist,
Being of soft, pure gold; and lace like mist
Needled in Venice for a princess gone,
All these he gave, and made her try them on.

And though her terror grew with all he gave,
She dreaded to refuse, and still he plied
The elegant bright things which women crave,
Given of old to some Imperial bride.
"But we'll return to gather these," he cried.
"There sounds the Nymph Dance; hurry back, my sweet.
The loveliest measure ever made for feet."

Lovely it was, that dance of outland men
Designed to music exquisite and old
To bring the nymphs and dryads from the glen
To dance with them by pen and lambing-fold
Swiftly the Emperor had her in his hold,
And tried to snatch a kiss and rushed her thence
Back to the mystic dance's turbulence.

Though dancing was her joy, she felt in this
That he, a forest-demon, had been brought
By divine music from that den of his,
To share a dance, though without human thought.
Bear-spirit, he, and she his victim caught . . .
The courtiers watched and sniggered, as she knew.
His red eyes glared, the dance's respite flew.

And at the end, the bear resumed his clutch
Again he dragged her to the treasure-room,
She terrified and shrinking from his touch,
He pressing near as menacing as doom.
He blew out all the lights, and in the gloom
He cried, "Now little Natalie, my own.
Here begins honeymoon for us alone."

She beat him from her, but he laughed and swore.
She prayed him by his manhood to let be.
He clutched her dress, which she in wrenching, tore.
She struck him in his face and struggled free.
"Nashy, I love you for your modesty,"
He said, with oaths, "Ecod, it suits you well.
Now listen here; you'd better not rebel . . .

Put modesty aside, and let us treat . . .
You little pudding, you're a dish so fair
A hermit saint would sell his soul to eat.
I'm not a hermit, but a rutting bear;
But I'm not selfish when I truly care.
I'll give you title, Duchess or Princess . . .
And such a wealth your Father will have less.

Dammee, my Nashy, I'm in earnest, now.
You show you love me, and I promise straight,
I'll guard and guarantee you and endow
Against whatever accident or fate.
I'll settle you a mansion and estate
And any rank and standing that suffice. . . .
Ecod, you're cunning . . . well, then, name your price . . .

Name anything you like that I command.
Half Russia, if you wish, half Asia, too,
With subject slaves as many as the sand
And jewels many as the morning dew.
All that I am and have, I offer you.
You cunning little slut, my modest miss . . .
My tempting Nashy, now I'll have a kiss . . ."

He rushed, but she as swiftly plucked a chair
Between them, that he tripped and nearly fell.
He snatched and tore the star out of her hair
And followed raging like a hound of hell,
Less like a hound in cry than one in yell.
"I'll teach you manners, Nashy, and be sure . . .
If you've another love, he'll find a cure . . .

Sailor or soldier, he shall stand aside.
Come here and yield or by my Russian crown,
Before to-morrow midnight, he'll have died
And you will be the clog that dragged him down.
I'll have you whipped at cart-tail through the town."
He caught her here: a brightness changed the gloom.
Some officers with lights were in the room . . .

The Emperor swore, released the girl, and raged.
The officer in charge with bended head
Replied "Your Majesty, the scene is staged . . .
The Russian Fleet is waiting to be sped.
Soon as the thousand rockets have been shed,
They will away . . . they wait for you to fire.
The Empress bade us wait on your desire."

Czar Peter cursed; the officer stood bowed.
Natalie stood in silence, shedding tears,
Out on the Palace Quay she heard a crowd
Blessing the Fleet with hymning and with cheers.
And answers from the Fleet came to her ears.
Michael was yonder, waiting to be gone.
"I'll fire the sign," the Czar said, "March. Lead on."

The lights withdrew, an ensign slammed the door,
Natalie in the dimness stood alone
Hearing them passing down the corridor;
She prayed to Death to take her for his own.
All her delightful heart was turned to stone.
A secret door swung open in the wall.
"Quick, Little One," she heard a woman call.

A lantern shewed; she looked not nor replied.
Her ruined life was all that she could see.
A woman suddenly was at her side,
A lady crowned, the Empress; it was she.
In dread of death she sank upon her knee.
The kindest voice in Europe said, "My dear,
There's still a safety for you; have no fear . . .

I have a carriage here to take you home.
Slip out from thence, and fly, not saying where.
Make for a nook where people never come
Let not your very parents know your lair.
Pursuit will follow, sure as flowers are fair,
Ruthless pursuit, but courage, little rose,
Come, quickly now, take hiding, and lie close."

Gently, the Empress held and led her thence.
"Courage," she said, "I, too, have suffered, child.
Ruin and misery and insolence,
And hope annulled and innocence defiled.
Finding you gone, the Czar will be as wild
As raging wolves, but let him thunder still.
Vow to escape, and I believe you will."

So helping and encouraging, she led
Into a passage by the secret door.
By stairway to the Palace grounds they sped.
The thousand rockets shattered with a roar.
The Navy cannon bade farewell to shore . . .
Michael had sailed; a carriage waited there.
"Go fast," the Empress said, "Tell no one where."

The driver shook his horses into speed
Empress and lighted Palace fell away,
Soon, Natalie was home in very deed,
Hastily tearing off her ball-array,
And putting on rough country woollens gray,
Staff, scrip and gold she took; then forth she stole,
Into the darkness, trembling to the soul.

None saw her go; she dared not leave a word;
Whither on earth to turn she scarcely knew,
More than the summer-fledgling swallow-bird
When autumn spider-webs are gray with dew;
But in her mind, she saw a faithful two,
Her foster-parents who would be her stay.
Michael had seen the man that very day.

"Down by the Docks" her love had met the man
He said not when, but still, that very eve.
He, with the timber-waggons and the van
(Yellow, with blue roof) of the forest-reeve.
Surely, that timber-wright would never leave
Until the Fleet had wandered down the tide
And the last star of the last rocket died.

He might be there, still watching, with his teams.
If he were there, her safety would be sure
From this mad Minotaur's impulsive dreams
To muzzle, nuzzle and trample on the pure.
If he were gone, the Baltic held the cure,
The swift green current setting Michael west
Would end her dread with very quiet rest.

Quaking, she hurried down the ill-lit roads
Into the unlit quarter of the Docks
By white, pine-scented stacks of timber-loads
And skeletons of ships upon the stocks.
The water leaking at the gates of locks
Lamented by her, and at every yard
She dreaded the night-robber or the Guard.

Then, suddenly, in front of her, she heard
Horse-bells and horses, and the drivers' cries.
Round the road-corner moving lights appeared,
With whip-cracks like to dropping musketries.
With grince of axle and the chink of tyes
The timber-waggons neared; she crouched and prayed
That forest-friend might help a frightened maid.

Team after team, the four-horsed waggons went,
The drivers strode beside, cracking their lashes,
The lanterns on the shafts a glimmering sent,
Now here, now there, a light in jerking flashes,
The puddles shone and spurted into splashes
Then darkness followed, then another team
With bells and strain swam up into the stream.

All passed; her foster-father was not there;
Or else had passed unseen; now all were gone.
She stood alone and wept in her despair
While overhead the stars wheeled slowly on;
Then, round the bend, another lantern shone
A whip cracked and a trotter's bells were ringing.
Her foster-father's self drew nearer, singing.

Jingling and swaying came the living-van
Last of the convoy, bringing up the rear
Proshka himself, her foster-mother's man,
Singing that brown Marfenka was his dear.
She, piteous, plucking courage, tottered near,
And called his name; he halted and leaped down.
"You, Miss," he said, "At night . . . this end of town?"

Swiftly she stammered out her great distress.
"My little child," he said, "My Wife's within,
My Daughter, too; come, Marf . . . Olushka . . . dress . . .
Here's our beloved sweet, Miss Natalin."
The women hurrying out soon plucked her in
In to the warm safe living-van, and there
Defied the Czar to touch her; let him dare.

As they went jingling onwards to the wood,
Natalie told them of the risks she brought.
As sure as daylight she would be pursued
And only shame awaited her when caught.
And royal vengeance would be surely wrought
On all found helping her to get away.
Marfenka said, "We'll save you, darling May.

By great good luck, the waggons are ahead
You must lie close within this living-van,
Out in the forest we will find a stead
Out of the way of even a forest-man.
If soldiers search us, listen: I've a plan
To outwit them; for, hark, Natasha dear
We have been spirit-smugglers many a year.

Out in the forest, we have private stills
And make the spirit, lusty and good store.
We run it into town when fortune wills
Hid underneath this waggon's secret floor.
If soldiers come a raging like the boar
You lying hidden where the puncheons lie
May sleep in quiet till the peril's by.

If, as I think, we scape the first pursuit,
You will be far in forest and secure;
Myself or Olga with you as may suit;
However long your trouble may endure.
A joy to us, beloved one, be sure;
But trust to us, whatever may impend.
To love you is our joy until we end."

Thus the good foster-mother cheered the child.
They put her into Olga's bed to rest
And all night long strode on into the wild
Unpeopled, uncut forest of the west
Where the red squirrel built his twiggy nest
And she-wolves littered underneath the thorns
And wild bulls gashed the tree-bark with their horns.

When morning came, they were within the wood
They halted to take counsel and break bread;
The luck of the escaper had been good
The timber-waggons still were well ahead.
Now came the happy daylight, bringing dread;
They dared not let their darling shew her face
Outside the van, from terror of the chase.

But Proshka said "Beyond the timber-camps
There are snug nooks where no one ever goes
Not even thieves, nor anchorites, nor tramps,
Nothing but wild-duck and the dappled does.
If once we get her into one of those
All may be well, but till we get her there
Let her lie close and let us all beware."

They lifted up the planking of the floor;
And snuggled Natalie on rugs within
The hollow of the smuggled spirit-store.
In quiet comfort she lay prone within;
Then on they went, but soon they heard the din
Of soldiers' bugles blowing near the wood,
It meant pursuers in all likelihood.

It was pursuit, for when the rockets failed,
When the last "Loath to lose you" had been blown,
And fading lights shewed where the Navy sailed,
The Czar returned, to find his fancy flown.
Her parents said, "She has gone home alone . . .
Mourning her lover, Michael, now at sea."
"Tell her, I'll visit her at dawn," said he.

They hurried home, to find their daughter gone.
At dawn, the Czar was shouting at the door.
"Now, little slut, Mock Modesty, come on . . .
What do you keep your Ruler waiting for?"
They told him "She is gone"; he stamped and swore.
"You've hidden her," he cried. "Go, find her out . . .
Or English as you are, you'll have the knout.

I say, you've hidden her, and shall produce
Or else I'll have you skinned and stuffed with straw."
He searched the house and thundered his abuse
And threatened every death by every law.
But still, the bird was fled out of his claw.
"I'll find her still," he blustered as he went.
"And you who've hidden her shall soon repent."

Galloping back, he ordered out his Horse
A squadron strong by every City Gate,
To follow, capture and bring back by force
The girl Natasha, danger to the State
Who may have left the City very late
The night before, or now might try to leave;
They were to seek and follow and retrieve.

Throughout the City, he proclaimed reward
In current coin, a thousand sequins, gold.
To anyone who brought her into ward
Or knew her present whereabouts and told.
She was a traitor, to be brought to hold;
And burying alive should be the pay
Of all who helped her and would not betray.

Then thinking of the phrase her parents used:
"Mourning her lover, Michael, now at sea."
He swore. "The little cat . . . I am abused . . .
That's where the little minx contrived to be.
She's with her lover, sailing to be free . . .
Aboard her Michael's ship; but I've a chance
To stop those happy lovers in their dance."

Instantly therefore he despatched in chase
Two swift pataches under press of sail
'Gallant and royal, stretching sheet and brace,
To catch and stop the squadron without fail,
And drag the flying lovers back to jail.
He promised both the captains they should rue it
Until their death-days if they failed to do it.

Then an espy-all reached him with a clue.
Natalie's parents, questioned to the bone,
About the friends their daughter trusted-to,
Had both agreed; "Her foster-kin alone."
And other questioning had made it known
That these, the foster-kin, were foresteers
In town that very midnight at the piers.

"Another thing," he said . . . But the Czar screamed
"That's where the little baggage ran to hide.
Gallop, now, Guards . . ." and out the lancers streamed,
They took Natasha's parents as their guide.
"She's gone into the forest," Peter cried . . .
"I'll have her now; her foster-folk shall swing."
The baffled spy cried, "Lord . . . another thing."

Out of the City gate the lancers strode
Into the forest, on the waggon's track,
Czar Peter cursed them forward as he rode
And threatened both her parents with the rack.
"You knew of this; when I have brought her back
Lord, sir, your English marrow-bones shall pay
Blood for the insolence of this delay."

Onwards these hunters galloped through the wood;
And now, ahead, the yellow van their mark.
The bugles blew, the Emperor hallooed,
And Natalie with terror quaked to hark.
A Captain gave a military bark
And Proshka stopped; the Czar, with all his men
Circled the waggon with a living pen.

"Come out, you little drab, you Natalie,"
The Czar, dismounting, shouted; "Out, I say.
You dolted woodman, answer. Where is she?"
Her Mother cried, "It is the Czar; obey."
Natalie heard her Mother as she lay,
But did not stir; Marfenka faced the task.
"What is Your Glory seeking, may I ask?"

Natalie's mother said, "We think our child
Ran to take shelter with you, being scared."
Marfenka said, "Why, no such luck," and smiled.
She oped the door and shewed the waggon bared.
"Search it," the Captain said; a sergeant stared.
"There's no one there." "Well, get inside and see,"
Czar Peter said. "Come out here, Natalie."

No answer came. Two lancers entered-in
They poked the bunks and rattled on the wall,
Opened the bread-barge and the flour-bin,
And lifted Marfa's hanging hat and shawl.
Then they reported, "No one, Sir, at all."
The devil in the Czar's eyes glittered wild.
He turned on Marfa, Proshka and their child.

"Where have you hidden her, you dog and slut?"
"Glory, we haven't seen her since the snow."
"All your three throttles shall be surely cut
If once you lie to me, so now you know.
I say, you've hidden her." "Your Glory, No."
"Now, on your duty, as you prize your skin.
She never prayed to you to take her in?

She never came to you last middle night,
Saying, 'Oh, hide me; oh, for pity, save'?
I know your mother-love has mickle might.
I can respect the love that makes you brave."
Marfenka whitened for the case was grave,
She knew too instantly her Ruler's mind
This last caressing was to make her blind,

To deceive Proshka and beguile her girl.
"Your Glory, all last night and all to-day
We've sorrowed that we never saw our Pearl, . . .
We brought a load of wood and came away, . . .
Lord, will you let my Darling's Mother say
Why she was scared and why she had to run?"
Czar Peter said, "I'll try another one . . ."

He lightened upon Proshka, who still stood,
Beside the horse. "You woodman, hearken here."
Proshka looked bright-eyed from his face of wood.
"When saw you last this foster-daughter dear?"
"Lord, in the frost, about the turn of year."
"The fifth of January," Olga said.
"Leaving the City, why were you delayed?

You are in charge of all a convoy's teams,
Yet here you are alone, your convoy, where?
You lingered in the City as it seems
To hide this baggage in some secret lair.
Where did you put her; turn and take me there."
"Your Glory," Proshka said, "We lingered on,
Down by the docks, after the men had gone,

First, to make sure that none had slipped away
Into the taverns, as they sometimes will,
Next, while we watched the squadron in the bay
Seeing the guns flash and the rockets spill.
We couldn't come away till all was still."
"You couldn't come away till she was hid.
You hid the trollop . . ." "No, Lord, God forbid."

The Czar lifted his whip as though to slash:—
"I tell you, dog, you hid her, and you lie.
You three shall all be knouted into mash."
But here he saw another track to try.
"You bribed a boatman where the wherries ply
To put her in her lover's ship, you hound.
And now she's with the squadron, outward bound . . ."

He turned on Olga. "Isn't that the fact?
Didn't you help her to her lover's ship?"
"Never, your Majesty, by word or act.
We left a load of timber at the slip
We watched the rockets from the lumber-tip,
Then started back; we neither saw nor heard
My foster-sister, neither glimpse nor word."

Czar Peter puckered at her with grim eyes.
"That sounds like truth," he said, "but all the same,
Men are the playthings of a woman's lies."
He glowered upon Proshka and his dame.
Then suddenly a new suspicion came
Into his mind, that Natalie had fled
Among the timber-waggons, on ahead.

"Mount, men," he said; he gave a parting threat
"If you assist your Natalie, or hide,
Well, burying alive is what you'll get.
So let this little warning be your guide.
Your convoy's on ahead? Good. Forward. Ride."
The lancers shipped their lances, closed their ranks,
And kicked their heels into their horses' flanks.

Yet, trotting off, they often turned to stare
(Czar Peter most) with grim, suspicious thought
That somehow Natalie was hidden there,
Though they had rummaged and discovered nought.
The side-arms clanked, the little horses fought
Against the bits, and so they topped a rise.
Then Marfa spoke. "Look out, now, for surprise.

Watch, Olga, if they turn. Within-van, quick."
She roused Natasha from her hidden bed,
With "Get to covert where the brush is thick,
Flat on the ground, and never lift your head.
Get out the nose-bag; let the horse be fed.
Czar Peter will return to bother more.
Someone will tell him we've a secret floor."

Natalie crept into the scrub, and lay
Prone in a little hollow of the ground;
She watched the patient insects on their way:
Her foster-folk ate dinner (by the sound)
Until the clatter of their spoons was drowned
By sudden horse-hooves; Peter had returned
As Marfa had expected, having learned.

"Listen, you dogs," he said, "and tell me true.
You smuggle spirits in a secret bin.
Open your van, unfasten and undo,
That's where you put your foster-daughter in
And if she's there, I'll skin you from your skin,
Each one of you, in public, in the Square
And nail you to the palings being bare."

Proshka said, "Lord, we have indeed a place
Inside the living-van, beneath the floor.
I'll open up the planks to shew your Grace."
He lifted, and displayed a woodman's store.
Some salted fish, some horse-beans, nothing more
Except two bottles of their home-made gin,
And one of mead; no trace of Natalin.

"So," Peter said, in guile, "she isn't here.
You, Madam, set us hunting a false scent."
He searched the woodman's face for signs of cheer,
On Proshka's wooden face no comfort went.
Then Peter's glare upon the women bent.
Marfenka, screening Olga with quick wit,
Said, "Glory, will you drink? Will you permit?"

The Glory deigned, Marfenka poured a dram;
Czar Peter on the parents bent his brows.
"These foster-parents haven't got your lamb.
God help you, if she's hidden in your house.
Here's to Natasha in a Russ carouse."
He drank his dram; Natasha's Mother said,
"Lord, never doubt my Natalie is dead."

Then, slipping from her horse, she fell in swoon.
Czar Peter cursed: "These women are a pest,
Bedevilled by their feelings and the moon.
Help her within the van and let her rest.
This is but the beginning of the quest.
Back to the City, quick, and hitch the van
With those spare horses, Captain Overman."

Back to the City streets they clattered straight,
Leaving Natasha lying in the wood
Sick for her parents' anguish at her fate
And full of terror in the solitude,
While nothing in her future promised good,
"And oh," she muttered, "would I could contrive
To tell my darling Mother, I'm alive."

This could not be, nor did the wood-folk dare
By any sign to let her parents know
That she was living and was hidden there.
Back to her parents' house they had to go
And watch the lancers search it, top to toe.
Till the Czar cursed them with "You linger long.
Get back, you, to the woods where you belong."

As they returned, Marfenka spoke her mind.
"No one must know, her parents least of all.
It will be certain ruin to be kind,
One silly word may bring about her fall.
Three foresters the less, the loss is small,
That's the result to us, of one word spoken.
But, to our darling, it's her whole life broken."

At dusk, they reached the thicket where she hid;
They camped, and all night guarded her in turn.
Then, in the morning, though no risks betid,
Nor lancers shewed, from what they might discern,
Knowing what any carelessness would earn,
They hid their darling in the secret nook
Under the floor, and so, departure took.

At noon, before they reached their journey's end
A sergeant's guard of lancers ringed them round.
The sergeant said, "Come . . . Open up here, friend.
A lovely girl is lost who must be found."
He stared into the opened van and frowned.
"Well, not much lovely damsel there, I think.
But rumour says you wood-folk carry drink?"

"Ah, sergeant," Marfa said, "you know too much . . .
There's no deceiving you, I well perceive.
We have some spirit . . . will you taste a touch?
Yes, and your riders if you'll give them leave . . ."
"Life is a silly business, but why grieve"
(The sergeant said) "while lovely woman's pan
Offers prime spirit to a soldier man?"

He took the pannikin which Marfa filled.
"A health," he cried, "to Madam, Sir and Maid.
May friendship's holy flame be never chilled
And Heaven prosper the distilling trade.
And may a lover's debts be ever paid.
And may fair hostesses, with such bright eyes
Bless every soldier sergeant till he dies."

He drank, and praised the spirit, then all drank
While the drink lasted; Marfa told the tale
Of the Czar's searching them; they reformed rank
The sergeant called, "Come on, my coats of mail.
And you, fair hostess, how the Czar could fail
To love you, having seen, is past belief.
Now, Madam, come; you'll have to see the Chief."

Marfenka quaked that something was suspect
Observed, betrayed, or ordered by the Czar.
She smiled upon him though her hopes were wrecked.
"Surely . . ." she said, "will that be very far?"
"No, over yonder, where the pennons are,
That's where the Chief 'll shoot you, all the three.
But, courage, hostess, leave the case to me. . . .

He'll have your waggon marked and let you go."
He led the waggon to a forest clearance
Where tethered horses whickered in a row,
And presently a Colonel made appearance,
All medals and moustache and interference.
He said, "What? What? Who are these fellows, hey?
Why, in the name of devils, can't you say?

Is this the girl? What? What?" The Sergeant spoke:—
"Lord, we have searched the waggon and these three.
He is a wood-reeve of the logging-folk
Examined yesterday by Majesty . . ."
"Well, what's the use of bringing them to me?
If you've examined them and found them clear?
Why, in the name of devils, bring them here?"

"Lord, if your Honour granted them a chit
The other wood-patrols would pass them through . . ."
"Why should they pass? I see no need of it . . ."
"The timber-reeve has marking-work to do."
"Get one from Sergy, then; get out here, you . . ."
With pass affixed, the wood-folk with their daughter,
Led the van woodwards from the men of slaughter.

So on, into the thicker of the wood,
On, to the timber-markers' camp they went,
By budding green, the dainty roebucks' food,
And leafy mould by beech-trees over-pent.
Where the red squirrel jabbered his content,
They halted, and released their Natalie
From the cramped coffin of her prisonry.

By moonlight, Proshka loaded up a cart
From loggers' stores, of plank and builders' gear,
The owls of after midnight saw him start
Deep into thickets no man trod for fear;
Within them was a reed-surrounded mere
Seen by him once when on a wood-survey
Towards that solitude, he took his way.

A tongue of dry land, cloaked by springing reeds
And by abundant boxwood overgrown,
Thrust to the lake exactly to his needs,
For mortals there were utterly unknown.
The sentinel blue heron stood alone
And did not stir for him; the wild-duck fed;
The swan glid by him, never turning head.

There, in the evergreen dry box, he made
A little wooden hut, with sloping roof,
Ditched all about for dryness with the spade,
And caulked with pine-pitch to be water-proof.
When he had finished, Proshka stood aloof
At many points, to see what could be seen
And then disguised it well with brown and green,

With paint, and broken reed and smears of clay
Pitching and mud he hid it from the sight,
Till nothing shewed of it that might betray.
Strong bars he shaped, to bar the door at night.
With needles of the fir two beds he dight.
Later, his Wife and he in darkness brought
Natalie safely to the shelter wrought.

The wise Marfenka told them of her plan:
She, or her daughter, or the two, would share
Natalie's hut, while Proshka kept the van
And brought them stores when happy chances were;
For some few weeks the living would be bare
And full of danger, but by keeping close
In constant watch, they might escape their foes.

There Proshka left them in the little hut,
A blanket and a little bread they had;
A wooden bar to keep the door well-shut;
No fire and no light to make them glad;
But terror plentiful to make adrad;
The forest full of soldiers, and the fear
Of spirits of the waste and of the mere.

Marfenka also had her private dread
Of troops molesting Olga; of her man
Giving some clue with brandy in his head
To some shrewd searcher coming to the van:
Of some chance track a forester might scan
And follow, to the hut, for well she knew
All tracks attract where passers-by are few.

Then, women in the loggers' camp would note
And talk about, all movers to and fro.
Night may be starless in her inky coat
But none so black that gossip cannot know
Who treads the night and whither he does go;
The lightest gossip in a lancer's ears
Might make them fourfold victim to the spears.

And well she knew what fury of pursuit
Would fill the forest while the ruler raged,
She knew his nature, having game afoot,
Not easily was Peter's wrath assuaged
Search up and down and crosswise would be waged,
And they, however careful they might be,
Could not so hide but somebody might see.

The first days passed, with very little food.
Then the two women ventured to set snares,
And search for birds' eggs in the reeds and wood,
And angle fishes in that lake of theirs
One shocking fright they had and many scares.
Three lancers passed them close yet never saw
As they lay huddled in the hazel-shaw.

And every night, the forest noises scared:
The owls with many cries, each cry a dread.
The footsteps of the unseen things who fared
The forest darkness as they quaked abed.
The steps which reached the door and ceased to tread,
And then the breathing of the thing that stood
Testing for weakness in that shed of wood.

After a week, Proshka brought news and stores:
The lancer searchers were recalled to base
The two might come more freely out of doors,
Yet not expect an ending of the chase,
A rumour spread abroad in every place
That Natalie had given them the slip
And now sailed westward, in her lover's ship.

Proshka had heard the naval shipwrights say
That certainly despatch boats had been sent
After the Fleet, with wet sheets, down the bay,
To catch the flying lovers as they went.
But this, the seamen said, was lust mis-spent,
No boats could catch the ships, which now were driving
West, ever west, the Baltic billows riving.

For weeks, Marfenka kept her darling trust
Close in the thicket by the water-side,
Denying herself bread, both crumb and crust,
So Natalie, her loved one, were supplied.
Starvation would have had them both for bride
When eggs had ceased and fruit was not yet red,
And fishes bit not, had not fortune sped.

They saw a withered tree collapse; they found
The coffer of its trunk, smashed open, filled
With wild bees' honeycomb a hundred pound
In rough wax heaps of golden Junes distilled.
This wealth they gathered-in and little spilled,
Then, as the chase relaxed, they ventured more,
And helped by Proshka built a winter store.

He gathered bricks and builded them a stove,
He brought them forest-pelts of wolf and bear,
And many a gummy branch they cut and clove
And many a fish they dried for winter fare:
Marfa or Olga, one was always there,
Whichever stayed with Proshka at the van
For Natalie alone thought, stitched and span.

Their simple heart's devotion made a wall
About their darling, to defend and save.
They dared not commune with her friends at all.
Her parents both supposed her in her grave,
Thrust in some ditch or tumbled in the wave,
Marfenka dared not let the tiniest word
Pass, of her life, lest it be overheard.

Her grieving parents mourned for her as dead;
In memory, a marble cross they raised.
The girls, her friends, some tears of sorrow shed,
And all her gentleness of beauty praised.
In generous young hearts an anger blazed
Against the Czar; but living still went on
The world resolved, that Natalie was gone.

Meanwhile, in daily dread of being found,
Natalie dwelt amid the forest-kind,
Crouched like the hare in terror of the hound
And yelling huntsmen cheering to the find.
Often she wept till she was nearly blind
For Michael gone, her parents and her friends
And young life's golden cord in broken ends.

Then, as she watched the courage and the love
Of those strong souls, her faithful foster-kin,
She trod her sorrow down and stood above,
And on her darkness saw a day begin;
Nothing's so lost that courage cannot win,
And she by love and strength was so immewed
Her very soul went out in gratitude.

There were these woodfolk risking life and limb
To save her, without question, without care
Filling her cup with love up to the brim.
Whatever Earth's romantic lovers dare
They did and outdid daily everywhere
Out of the fire of the truth and seeing
That burned upon the hearth-stone of their being.

How could she thank where nothing could repay?
All in her power was to give delight
In cheerfulness in labour of the day
In thoughtfulness at coming-on of night,
In thankfulness that never could requite
The simple love like very fire pure,
Like sea-wind wholesome, like the granite sure.

Still, there was ever much that she could do
To save the three from labour, cold and wet,
Wood she could gather, woodland herbs to brew,
Berries and nuts to seek for, bread to set,
Fish to beguile for store, with line or net,
The walls to caulk with moss, and plans to make
Against the winter, sickness, or mistake.

Always the coming to and from the shed
By those three foster-friends was done at night
From different directions, and in dread,
Of woodwives with less charity than sight.
And after dark no fire and no light
Shewed in the hut, but all was shuttered close.
The scarlet hips replaced the fallen rose.

The harvest moon shone upon autumn-time,
Grey veils of spider web the brambles bore,
The grasses after dawn were crisp with rime;
Ice whitened upon puddles near the shore.
The birds flew southward and were seen no more;
The squirrel, having garnered his last nut,
Went to his den and saw the door was shut.

The leaves blew down; the ruts upon the ways
Hardened like rock with ice; then came the snow
The many-dropping murderer who slays
With touch so soft his victims hardly know.
It drifted deep where Natalie lay low
With one or other of those women two.
Now winter was, another dread they knew.

For in the winter, courtiers sometimes rode
To rouse and shoot the winter-sleeping bears;
Crushed was their covert, now that it had snowed
Plain to the passer stood that hut of theirs;
Dark among whiteness, open to the airs
With footprints leading to it; what more clear
Than, that a sportsman, seeing, would draw near?

Open to every quarter lay the hut
That summer-long had hidden in the brake;
At any moment men might come to cut
A summer-store of ice-blocks from the lake.
Natalie Maisie could but inly quake
Knowing that any passer-by would see
The shed or smoke and ask "Whose can it be?"

Yet, though she sometimes heard a distant shot
And once the cry of ban-dogs at a bear,
No hunter chanced upon that lonely spot,
Nor did the ice-men come a-cutting there;
But in the full-moon nights, the frosty air
Rang with the cry of wolves and the sick bleat
Of something hunted failing on his feet.

And once, at midnight, shots and shouts and screams
Rang through the wood, not very far away,
Going to door, she saw the fire-gleams
Pistol on pistol-shot, from some affray
Then horse-hoofs and the belfry of a sleigh
Crossing the vale below her, out of sight,
Then silence, and an owl-call and the night.

At dawn, she and her foster-fellow stole
Out to the thickets where the noise had been
And found a dead man at a fir-tree bole
Shot in the heart; a robber by his mien;
The tramplings in the snow displayed the scene,
Riders had chased a sleigh out of the road;
There they had fought, and one of them abode.

The women quaked lest brothers of the gang
Should seek their fellow and observe their trace,
But robber wisdom lets the dead go hang.
They left their comrade quiet in his place
Death, unlike life, put peace upon his face
The wolves devoured him, and heavy snow
Covered the spot, if any came to know.

Slowly, the northing Sun recovered strength,
The trees dripped in the day-time from the thaw,
Pools opened in the water, till at length
The lake was one blue mirror without flaw;
Mud reappeared and sledges would not draw,
Some shy birds sang, awaking dormice yawned
The croaking marshes told that frogs had spawned.

Then in warmth of rain the spring began,
The buddings split their covers and were green,
Daily the hider had less dread of man,
Daily more leafage covered up the scene;
Soon, she was secret as a fairy queen
By haunted oak upon a moonbeam riding;
A year had passed since she had taken hiding.

Meanwhile, the Navy made the western cruise,
Southward, away, into the shining bright
Blue tropic water that the dolphins bruise
And silver flying-fishes streak with light;
They anchored in the Scarlet Logwood Bight
And changed their northern wares for precious wood,
Then turned for Russia from that solitude.

On coming-in, men boarded Michael's ship
Sent by the Czar to look for Natalie,
Some of the frigate's grommets had to strip
To make the searchers certain none was she.
A miserable coming home from sea
To find his darling gone, himself suspect.
Her parents told him how his life was wrecked.

They never doubted Natalie was dead
Her pitiful last moments were unknown
But she was gone, her burial service read
Her record cut on a memorial stone.
He as a half-thing, loveless, left alone,
Stood as one stunned, that his imagined wife
Was only memory, long since gone from life.

Her parents took him up into her room
A shrine kept sacred to a saint revered,
Curtained, one taper burning in the gloom,
Still as she left it when she disappeared.
Each little thing by bitter grief endeared;
The red rose spilled, the necklace last in use,
The cloak flung down, the two white dancing shoes.

Beyond all question, Natalie was dead.
He mourned and wept for her and knew despair.
Her beauty's image never left his head;
Waking or sleeping, she was ever there.
Meanwhile, he unrigged ship and left her bare,
Discharged of logwood, gunless, stripped of pride,
Like to himself now Natalie had died.

Then the Czar's orders came, that all aboard
Should come ashore, to learn what other strands
Complete the perfect seaman's ninefold cord,
In long-established fleets in foreign lands.
To work in rope-walks or as dockyard hands,
In sail- or rigging-lofts, or with the founders
Casting the gun-decks' two and thirty pounders.

Michael was ordered to the building-slips,
Thence to the forests with a timber-gang,
To mark the planks and timbers fit for ships,
In the dim greenness where the giants sprang.
The ringing of the barking-irons rang
In many a falconed grove of mighty trees
Whose stars had destined them to sail the seas.

When all the season's ringing had been done,
He and two friends were ordered to explore
The outer forests visited by none
To note what naval wood their thickets bore.
One day their chief allotted and no more;
One, north, one, south, and Michael, to go west,
And none to lose himself, was the behest.

So Michael, taking horse to ride alone,
Asked for some guidance from the forest-reeves,
Who said, "This westward forest is unknown,
Save to the wolves and bears and hunted thieves."
Dark with foreboding was that world of leaves
To Michael setting-forth; he called good-bye,
Then entered in, and branches hid the sky.

Summer had set her silence on the birds,
Already, here and there, a leaf was gold.
One distant drilling pecker jarred his girds,
Before him, wood-mice flitted under mould,
He trotted forest timbered big and old,
The pigeons sometimes made his cheek aghast
Clacking from tree-tops after he had passed.

Riding, he noted well the sorts of trees,
Their growth and goodness and what chances showed
Of timber-waggons coming there with ease,
And getting back to City with the load.
The timber ever bettered as he rode.
He noticed it, although he did not care
He was but conscience working in despair.

Some goodly oak-trees drew him from his course,
These he would plot before he trotted east;
He turned towards them, envying his horse
That lived by corn and slumber as a beast
Himself was living after life had ceased;
Thus sorrowing, he reached a space of grass
Where overhead he saw some wild-duck pass.

And scarcely had the ducks gone necking by
When, lo, a willow-plot, with reed-stalks shedding
And herons flogging from him with a cry
And white swans clanking upward from their steading
And, lo, an unexpected lake was spreading
Edging the course by which he meant to pass.
A fish's snout ringed ripples in its glass.

A headland, dense with cover, jutted out
Into the lake, and in its reedy close
Someone unseen was dwelling, beyond doubt,
For from the scrub a breath of smoke arose
Faint as a chimney smoke when no wind blows,
Was it some fisher, or a killer fled
From Christian haunts because his hands were red?

Michael was wary, knowing that a shot
Might come before a hail from dwellers there;
Now as he neared it, he could see the cot
From which the smoke went up into the air
He shouted, lest he take them unaware
And seem an enemy; but none gave heed.
The silent smoke breathed up among the reed.

None answered; he approached, with lifted hand
Calling: "I come in friendship; do not fear."
A little path led to the jut of land
Beyond it lay the quiet of the mere.
The door-latch clattered as his horse drew near
The door swung open on a cottage dim
And Natalie herself stood facing him.

He slipped down from his horse, with "Natalie".
But still she stared, white-lipped and terrified.
Rough-clad and changed, she was; but it was she.
"How have you found me? Who has been your guide?
O, Michael, am I caught at last?" she cried.
"Not caught, beloved Natalie, but found
When all the world believes you killed or drowned.

How have you lived here? Who has sheltered you?
Whose hut is this? How did you find the place?
Can this have been your home the winter through?
Far from church-bells or any Christian face?
How have you managed to escape the chase?
The Emperor has a price upon your head . . ."
"Now you can earn it, Michael dear" she said.

You, who have suffered parting, will know well
What happiness those meeting lovers knew
And how a minute's heaven cancels hell,
And on what wings of flame the minutes flew
But in their joy, the question, what to do
Oppressed them both, and Natalie was sure
None but the Empress could their trouble cure

And even she might find the royal bull
No easy calf to guide into the pen;
Lust still might keep their tide of sorrow full,
And she still hidden from the world of men.
Marfoutka leading, guided Michael then
Into the tracks and thence he rode with speed
To kneel before the Empress and to plead.

He found the Empress in her theatre
Watching the flitting of her dancers' grace;
All forest-spattered still he knelt to her
And pled the horror of his darling's case.
She listened with a light upon her face.
"Come to the Czar" she said. "Your poor bird caged,
Need fear no more; he's otherwhere engaged."

She led him to the Czar and told the tale.
"Think, Peter mine," she said, "what she has borne,
Out in the wood, beyond the Christian pale
Living with forest-creatures all forlorn
Rather than stoop to be a thing of scorn.
And this young man, her lover has gone seeking
And now has found, which is a joy past speaking."

"Found . . . by a sailor, too," the Emperor said.
"So she is found; trust sailormen to find.
Well . . . I am glad . . . I feared that she was dead.
Beauty makes monarchs mad and passion blind.
She made a pretty fever in my mind . . .
And I was harsh, and she has had a year
Alone, in hell . . . What must I do, my dear?"

The Empress smiled. "Do, Peter mine," said she,
"Do like the Royal Prince you truly are.
Come to the forest, straight, and set her free,
And make her Fortune like a shining star.
You, who were grim, be, now, the glorious Czar.
Order your carriages and horses straight
Give, to her folk, their child, to her, a mate."

"Dammy, my beauty," said the Czar, "with you
I sometimes am a King; without you, no,
Nought but a drunkard lusting after brew.
A wild boar ramping and a cock in crow.
Beauty, you shame me; hurry, let us go.
We'll fetch her home; but, oh, my moon and sun,
Some other reparations must be done.

She shall be married in the chapel here
And she shall have the dowry of a queen,
And this young sailorman shall be a peer,
And Captain our Imperial Barquentine,
And Russia shall forget the beast I've been
And say 'This is a King'; come, Beauty, swift,
Now, sailor Michael, with a fair wind . . . shift.

But, stay, my Michael, first, I offer you
My shame, and my repentance and regret.
And any satisfaction that is due.
My whole heart's blood would never pay the debt.
Take, if you can, my hand, and let's forget.
Now, dammy, Beauty, come; we've shaken hands.
Now for this hermit in the forest lands."

They brought her home in the Imperial Car,
Natalie and the Empress, side by side,
Michael in triumph sitting by the Czar,
Who, a month later, gave away the bride.
He gave her dowry, house and place of pride;
To Michael, a promotion and a sword,
Active employ and thrice the pledged reward.

So, the young lovers' happiness began,
So, it increased in fortune till the end,
Nor did the Czar forget the forest-man,
Nor the two women, fosterer and friend.
Proshka had money, more than he could spend;
Marfa, the dairy-farm of her desire,
Olga, a dowry, when she wed the squire.

A Poet wrought a Ballet of the story,
A rare Musician set it to a Suite,
A Painter robed and mounted it in glory,
And starry Dancers blessed it with their feet.
When faces are again glad in the street,
When hatred is put off and has its pardon,
I hope to see it danced at Covent Garden.

PAVILASTUKAY

(The name is accented on the third syllable;
it is supposed to mean *Ruins in the Wood.*)

JONNOX was English, educated, male,
With private means, unmarried, thoughtful, travelled,
His country's many glories left him pale,
His country's many errors left him gravelled.
The evils of the Nations left him baffled,
But striving still to find some mental cure
For all the wickedness that men endure.

At first, he thought, "Pride in the sense of power,
That killer of the sympathies, the pride
That loves to see the victim cringe and cower,
That is the chief abominable guide . . .
As hunting men pollute a countryside
So statesmen stain the Nations with the arts
Which come from wooden heads and iron hearts."

Later, he thought, "A yet more fatal seed
Growing a heavier crop on blacker mud,
And podded in the rotting mind, is greed,
Greed sucking pennies from a brother's blood.
Greed that exacts the berry and the hud,
The leaf, the root, and then employs the Law
To wrest the very life with itching claw."

Later, he thought, "Stupidity alone
Is Man's destroyer, feebleness of brain,
That clings to silliness it should disown,
That worships silliness it should disdain,
That makes its god now Moloch and now Cain
Now Mammon, or with ninefold bitter hate
Of Man, the new totalitarian state.

The multitude of men, like will-less weevils,
Swayed by their ruling ministers, or class,
Will, like their rulers, suffer any evils
Rather than think; it therefore comes to pass
Tiger and tombstone rule the human ass,
Or the ass rules, and he who brays the loudest
His is the soul of whom the world is proudest."

Still, feeling sure that after long delay
The good beats down the worser and endures,
Jonnox, by speech and writing, day by day,
Attacked the evils and propounded cures.
He mocked at all the politicians' lures,
And at the many sops that so derange
The knife-edged purpose seeking for a change.

In speech and written tracts he did propound
The wickedness of cruelty and greed,
Based on injustice deep within the ground,
All bringing ill and making evil breed.
His countrymen took very little heed
He was a crank, they thought, the kind of curse
Who calls things evil when they might be worse.

Of all the many things that men abhor
The worst, comprising every ill in sum,
To Jonnox, was abominable war
The smiter of mankind in martyrdom;
And lest another shaking war should come
To shatter all the preciousness of men
Jonnox was eloquent with voice and pen.

At first, there seemed to him a tiny chance
That, after the last war, men might unite
Defending Man and his inheritance
From governmental total lack of light.
The dusky chance soon disappeared in night,
And Jonnox sighed and took it for a rule
That God's own image liked to be a fool.

But now he saw unscrupulous small bands
Make use of this discovery and seize
Their Nation's powers with their bloody hands
To turn the future whither they should please.
He thought, "Praetorian guards were such as these
Now the Augustan quiet comes to crash.
No light henceforth; just fire, smoke and ash.

While there are tigers, antelopes will die;
So much is clear; but this, that mature men,
Sharing a little glimmer of the sky
Should make their heritage a slaughter-pen,
And blast their penny comforts out of ken
Because a farthing scoundrel orders so,
Not thus do planets in their Heaven go.

No, they obey a ruling from the Sun
And sweep their starry orbits without clash
Roving the void and singing as they run
Obeying without dread of any lash.
Onward without reward those wonders thresh,
And Man a speck upon the least of note,
Gives his brief gasp to cut his brothers' throat.

Gone is all hope of European peace
The yapping bladder, and the bloody blade
That preached and started murder, cannot cease
Only by blood can murder be allayed,
Blood is their doctrine, spilling blood their trade;
And England knows that, unprepared as ever,
She, only, will resist them (or endeavour).

Searching the Press for comfort, he would find
The leaders saying "War is Nature's course.
As tiger ruins deer, the master-mind
Ruins the dodderer by use of force.
Nature abhors both pity and remorse,
And stamps out both" . . . still . . . Jonnox' thought remained.
"Man is not Nature, but a something gained. . . .

A something gained from Nature, at great cost,
By very great illusions somehow won,
And now in deadly peril to be lost
By darknesses' denial of the Sun . . .
When gods are false, O, seek another One,
Seek swiftly, seek, before all hope is dead."

Here, nervous breakdown brought him to his bed.

They gave him bromide and prescribed a rest,
Tonics with iron and a change of scene;
They said he was sub-consciously obsessed
By nineteen-hundred, fourteen to eighteen;
They gave injections culled from bine and bean
And many different glands, and then, away
They shipped him foreign for a holiday.

Although the threat of war made coming back
To men with any forethought, most unsure,
Jonnox embarked upon the eastward track
Across the ever tameless, ever pure.
He went to seek the sun and find a cure
Where tawny beggars ask for English pennies;
His shipmates played deck-quoits and table-tennis.

Europe, its climates and its costumes ceased;
In silvery haste the flying fishes swept
And still the ship strode on into the East
And still the table-tennis pipped and pepped.
Nightly, to negro noise, the jazzers stepped.
They reached Serak, their seventh port of call
And moored off Purovana's fortress wall.

Jonnox was told that they would fuel ship
There in the berth at any rate till four;
The passengers had time to take a trip
To see the cinemas or sports ashore;
There would be pony-racing; but a score
Of other lures were printed in the Guide.
This Jonnox read, to help him to decide.

He read that Spagha shooting might be good
In normal seasons, till the end of May:
That the bazaar's bright, coloured multitude
Of eastern silkwork was a rich display:
That at a place called Pavilastukay,
Deep in the jungle, to be reached by bus,
A ruined temple was thought marvellous.

Other delights were offered, but the rest
Were such as eastern tourists always meet.
To Jonnox' mind, the ruins seemed the best;
A dozen others thought them worth the heat.
Jonnox was sure, that to escape the beat
Of table-tennis balls for a few hours
Would strew the day with (figurative) flowers.

Straightway, the party went ashore to find
Conveyance to the ruins in the wood.
They cursed the bus because it had no blind;
They cursed the going, for the track was rude.
They cursed the beastly lunch of foreign food,
A sort of curried monkey, done with ghee.
Then forth they strode, to curse what they should see.

But coming forth into the blinding heat
To struggle through the jungle to the stones,
A distant noise of water sounded sweet
In Jonnox' ear; it stirred him to the bones.
A temple, with the gods upon their thrones,
Might be impressive, but in heat appalling
Jonnox was tempted by that water falling.

He asked the Guide, "Where is the waterfall?"
He, pointing, said "Him jungle; muchee thick."
Then Jonnox: "Can I get to it at all?"
The Guide: "Him stingee snake; him bitee tick."
The other tourists said "O, Jonnox; quick."
"Come," said the Guide, "but vellee little way . . .
Nice temple, see, of Pavilastukay . . ."

But Jonnox said, "No temple, thanks, for me.
If there's a river near, I mean to swim."
So, when the others went, he shewed a fee
To natives there that they should pilot him
Down to the water through the jungle dim
Which when they understood, they did, and bared him
A sight for which no guide-book had prepared him.

He reached a space through which a river flowed
Over a fall most exquisitely bright.
Clear-coloured marbles kept it in its road;
And hard beside, exulting in the light
A Palace stood, a thing of such delight
That Jonnox thought, "The temple of the Sun . . .
So here I am; there can be only one."

But, listening for pistol-shots and song,
His fellow-tourists' sign, and hearing nought
Save the cascade, he knew that he was wrong
This was no temple whither tourists sought.
No rideacock with guns instead of thought,
No guide-book writer, even, had been here.
None but the birds came hither year by year.

It had been hidden from the white man's eyes
Till then, perhaps; he, Jonnox, was the first.
The jungle-thrust had had it for a prize
Creeper and blossom had it all immerst.
But though the engulfing weed had done its worst
It did its best; no creeper could defile
That which Man's quickened soul had stamped with style.

So Jonnox, gazing, muttered "It is plain.
There was a City here; the Temple shewn
Must be but one of many that remain.
This that I see is utterly unknown.
For such a miracle of carven stone
Would bring a thousand tourists week by week
O miracle, if you could only speak."

The carven marble edged the river-side.
A fountain still miraculously played;
The roots had bursten many jointings wide
And cornices had fallen and decayed
But still a majesty of planning stayed
That said to Jonnox' soul from everything:—
"Man's spirit fashioned me to house her King."

The natives, who had brought him watched his face.
He thought "they have observed me; and they know
That I shall not betray this wondrous place
To tourist-folk who only come and go."
He asked the leader of the band to shew
A way into the ruins; the man pointed
A narrow, trodden breach through stones disjointed.

Still shaken by the splendour he beheld,
He clambered up the gapway in the wall
And gazed upon that monument of eld
In wavering shadow from the fountain-fall.
Some tiny deer who had no fear at all
Grazed on the courtyard grass; the buck raised head
And stared at Jonnox once but had no dread.

Some ribald monkeys talked, the fountain splashed:
Beneath the fall, the rainbows gleamed and faded;
Ospreys were fishing where the water lashed;
The parrots screamed and jangled as they raided;
The bubbles of the cataract abraded
Against the marble wall; the tiny deer
Wrenched at the grass, eyed Jonnox and drew near.

They moved aside for him as he descended
Into those courts of grass, so green and cool,
So living with the mind of someone splendid
Whom Time the enemy had put from rule.
The purple-blossomed creeper choked the pool
And had destroyed the fountains, save the one
Still tossing silver leafage at the sun.

Slowly, still marvelling, he crossed the grass
Towards the Palace, thinking "This was wrought
By men who never let Life's minute pass
But stretched their eager hands to it, and caught,
And pressed this glory from it, strength and thought
Working as one, to this undying thing
In praise of Man, Earth's only god and king."

Whichever way he turned, the City shewed;
The marble wharfings stood, where ships had lain;
Streets opened inland, all with ruin strowed;
The market shone with flowers bright from rain;
Then court on painted court began again,
With frescoed fables in the cloistered walks
Where now the birds plucked cherries from the stalks.

Often, in places where the encroaching wood
Had touched and clutched yet failed to overcome
Leaving a building perfect, Jonnox stood,
Expecting lovely citizens to come;
No footstep struck, each singing voice was dumb,
No citizens, save painted shapes were there,
But those he judged unutterably fair.

Sometimes, they were so beautiful, it seemed
That they were living, more than living, bright
As spirits from eternity who streamed
Out of their heaven into earthly light
Divinest fireflies in mortal night.
Perhaps, one of those splendid shapes might turn
Descend, and tell him all he longed to learn.

The fables seemed familiar; he could see
A woman helping as her limber lad
Struggled to take an apple from a tree
That was all dragon-kept and snake-bestad.
Fire and poison the scaled keepers shad
Yet up he climbed, and she with praises cheered
And beat the dragons from him as he neared.

Then was a scene which shewed the apple won
Plainly it brought no shadow of a curse;
No; but illumination of the Sun
Upon the wonders of the Universe.
They were as planets with the Moon for nurse
And starry creatures hymned them as they saw
World beyond world the glory of the law.

Then there were scenes which shewed the two, attended
By those bright creatures, fighting with the foes
Which wage on Man a battle never-ended:—
The mortal Sickness with the cure none knows,
Old Age and Poverty, and, King of those,
Stupidity in accident of rule
Dealing his death from being born a fool.

There was Stupidity with all his court,
The wooden head, the iron heart again,
The martial thing, all uniform and snort,
The legal thing, all parchment and disdain,
The cleric things, each carrying a chain,
The politician things, each yapping loud,
To subject apathy, the hopeless crowd.

Then followed paintings shewing them in rout
As customs inadapt to human needs,
And beauty came as wisdom drove them out
And hope sprang starry from her scattered seeds,
And hope brought faith in Man and lovely deeds
And lovely buildings fitted for the flower
Of Man, the spirit, living in his power.

The buildings in the paintings were in sight
Though ruined and bejungled they still stood
To prove that Man had lived in a delight
In spite of iron heart and head of wood . . .
The starry creatures had o'ercome the crude
Wonder had triumphed through the happy pair
The hero and the woman painted there.

He looked upon their faces, and abased
His head in awe from looking at the wise.
A man and woman, calm and eager-faced
With tranquil gladness looking from their eyes.
No cruelty, no greediness, no lies,
No treachery, no self, could wield a sway
While such were crowned in Pavilastukay.

Himself was standing where the two were shewn
Within the splendour they had holpen raise.
There, in the painting, was the carven stone
Just at his hand as in the ancient days
The gilding on its fruits had ceased to blaze
The traffic by its term was no more flowing,
The painting shewed it when the clock was going.

There they endured, portrayed for him to see
The city and her citizens of old
Men without any talk about to be
Or not to be, but excellently bold
In spirit to press on, to touch, to hold,
To bring into the world the shining thing
Joy's golden crownet upon Man the King.

"These, these," he muttered, "have discovered Life
These were not kinged by cannibals or dupes,
As in unhappy Europe, hell of Strife,
Where with red beak the hawk of rapine stoops
These had but Love and Joy, no other troops
If they believed in God, they believed more
In divine Man that divine Woman bore."

Knowing that what he saw had been attained
And might again be had, he trod the courts.
No face upon the walls was sad or pained,
Merry alike their toiling and their sports;
Lovely alike their work-place and resorts
In sunlight, by the river, among flowers,
Man's earthly life, but different from ours.

"This is a dream," he muttered, "I shall wake.
Life never has been thus; nor could be, ever.
Death murders all, and half the living break
From silly spite, the other half's endeavour.
And sickness nulls the strong, and age the clever,
And greed the grinder gnashes to enslave.
Such is our crawl from cradle to the grave.

Yet, what is dirtier crime than to deny
That what the best imagine may exist
By right direction of Man's energy?
One pluck of rein by some inspired wrist
And forth the stupid staggers from the mist
To laugh amid the lightning without fear
No longer planet-sick, but Zeus's peer.

These painted people all are nobly born
From splendid bodies filled with wit and grace,
Want never ground, nor sorrow made them mourn,
Tranquillity and joy are in each face
And there a Prince is in a builder's place
Laying a stone; and saving at the farms
Guarding the cattle, no-one carries arms.

No diseased body, no afflicted mind
Has wedded here; the stock is without flaw,
Examples of a perfect human kind
With Joy for bread and Excellence for law.
This stock has stablished what its thinkers saw.
Here supreme sight has gone with willing hand.
And life has crowned what inspiration planned.

No politicians here polluted air
With party cries; these spirits plainly knew
That if the citizens are fashioned fair
Fair dealing comes with little more ado.
And cruelty with all its filthy crew
Was banished hence; no male and female cannibals
Rode here to sport in cruelty to animals.

Since all were nobly born and taught and fed
They had from birth the instinct to excel
To make life fairer and to lift Man's head
And bring his butterfly out of his shell,
To give was more delightful than to sell
Within this City where a human sense
Was reckoned richer than a lot of pence.

To make life fair; to make it fairer still,
To banish Death was here the constant thought
The bending and the lighting of the will
Forever, here, that deep solution sought.
That wretched Man should not be victim caught
But spirit freed, as by the will he may
Or surely was, in Pavilastukay.

They fought with bad heredity, and won.
They fought with poverty and made it die.
They fought with all the insults to the Sun
Under the sceptre of stupidity.
They fought illusion, howsoever high
Of god or race or state, as fetters all
Making Man subject, keeping him in thrall.

Their weapons were but thoughts found in the brain,
This is the thing remarkable, that here
They conquered no-thought, and the marks remain
Though dimmed, as beauty excellently dear."
Thus did the frescoes that remained appear
To Jonnox as he trod that city's ways.
The deer, ignoring him, returned to graze.

"Death and his adjuncts were the things they fought"
He muttered, "Death, the enemy of life
They battled, having nothing but a thought,
One quaking blade of an unfinished knife
Man cannot yet be winner in the strife;
They did not win that oldest of all wars,
But they delayed Death's knocking at the doors."

Deep in an alabastrine court, wherein
No art-irrupting root had yet begun
Though butterflies and sunlight entered in,
He found a painting like the living sun.
"This is the loveliest painting ever done,"
He said, amazed; for there upon the wall
Were children, going to a festival.

A hundred children going to a joy
Transcendent in delight but not revealed,
Some with balloons or flags or other toy
Or berried twigs or flowers of the field
Each in the sweetest gladness life can yield
Although the elders by that brook of youth
Smiled from a deeper joy in greater truth.

"O children, whither do you go?" he cried.
"O gladness, living once in souls of men,
Now only living while these walls abide
Betwixt the jungle and the river-fen,
Come as a sunlight into Man agen,
Let killing and the plots for killing stop,
And wisdom come from out her mountain-top.

This Palace and her City were not built
By State-owned serfs, State-captained to make slaves
By treachery, by blood and treasure spilt,
By hecatombs of corpses without graves,
But by a rapture, flooding-in in waves
From some great ocean waiting for the cry
From souls in deserts burnt under the sky.

Some leader here had wisdom and gave call
Then his disciples cried, and soon, oh soon
The joy of some was the delight of all
And all souls carrolled like the birds in June.
Full Summer and full rapture and full moon,
And nothing starved and nothing warped by hate
Man's three foes quelled, false prophet, brigand, state.

Somewhere within these thickets of live green
So massed and tangled, are the tumbled bone
Of this the City that was Crown and Queen
Perhaps of all the cities Man has known.
They painted fair their gladness on the stone
And then went hence together, Joy and Power.
What death-bell tolled upon so fair an hour?

Ah me, what death destroyed this living hope?
It was not war; for warriors use fire
On men and things beyond their sorry scope.
Famine, perhaps, or fever from the mire;
Or did they trek away with bright desire
To reach some fabled town of Croatan
To dwell there still, unknown of other Man.

In Europe, when thought comes, the want of thought
Or want of thought in time, destroys it, sure.
The politicians mock the warnings brought,
The careless cry 'Our comforts will endure.'
The stupid say 'This thinking is a lure
To bring men into trouble'; and the lazy
Say 'All this worry about art is crazy.'

Little by little, what was tilled declines,
The money for the corn-field goes in shares,
A fungus spoils the fruit-trees and the vines,
But that is in the country, and who cares?
They build new blocks of flats in all the squares
And put up rents, and rates and taxes rise
And folly finds more followers than the wise.

Then state departments multiply in swarms
An army with old weapons or with none,
The others with their stacks of printed forms,
All thinking 'form filled-in is duty done.'
And when a building falls a worser one
Succeeds, and then a worse, and then a hut.
Then, an old cellar; then the shop is shut.

The end was sudden here; some mortal chance
Earthquake, infection, blight or insect-pest
Ruined the merriment and stopped the dance
And put the thinking under an arrest.
Earth's littlest killed her greatest and her best
The unexpected happened without warning
The Night came down and there was no more morning.

Thought could not reach the insect-carried germ
That killed, and so they perished in their prime;
For Nature is as happy with the worm
As with the brain triumphant and sublime.
But a belief in Man so splendours Time
That, centuries after, seeing men shall wonder.
Vision is lightning brief, and then the thunder.

Still, I have had this glimpse; and time remains
To study more . . ." but here a klaxon's bray
Came to his ears across the jungle-canes
Impatient busmen called their fares away
Again, again it blew; he could not stay
His native guide crying, "Tuan . . . oh . . .
De honourable bus he wantee go."

He hurried thence, but still the klaxon blew.
His fellow-tourists, tired, hot, athirst,
Cried, "Buck it, Jonnox; what's been keeping you?"
The driver and conductor scowled and curst.
They started back; and soon a tire burst
And darkness came, and as the planets shone
The guide remarked, "Me tinkee shippee gone."

It was not so; she stayed; they went aboard
A choleric Captain, chafing with delay,
Said, "You're the last consignment, by the Lord
To see the wreck of Pavilastukay.
You've wasted on us three good hours of day.
Now we've to run Perimba Strait at night;
And since the war-scare they've removed the light."

They were the last; the Company was told
That visits to the site delayed the ship.
The lunch-house shut up shop; the bus was sold,
No other purser advertised the trip.
The jungle reassumed its thwarted grip.
And like the jungle, war resumed its fetters
On war-delighting people and their betters.

Though reckoned rather frail to serve and die
Jonnox was amply strong enough to feel
The all-besetting, aching misery
In all the months of hatred, blood and steel
When common danger linked the commonweal.
He bore with folly, danger, grief and pain,
Thinking his thought "This must not be again."

When in his iron hat he trod his beats
Crunching at every step the fruits of strife,
The powdered brick and glass that had been streets,
And sad at the stupidity of life,
Then like the lifting thrilling of a fife
Within his mind that City's image thrilled,
Saying, "Much better things have once been willed.

Much better things, which can again be had
Will, therefore, to possess the life you saw
Of men and women perfect, children glad
Living at peace in cities without flaw.
The anarchy that makes itself the law
That must be killed before the holiday
Of cities like to Pavilastukay.

And since men covet change, and tiger-men
Are often born and often bring a change
To make men dwellers in the caves agen,
Well, reckon it unhappy, but not strange,
And in the cellar of the burnt-out grange
Or huddled in some drain amid decay
Still think there once was Pavilastukay,

Which can be had again, if there be will.
Pray not to any god for it, but plan
Imagine, work, determine, struggle still
That out of modern man there may come MAN.
Life was a sorry thing when it began
Life is a sorry thing when warrings sway.
But Life was fair in Pavilastukay.

Therefore, come any devilry devised
By things called soldiers serving things called states,
Destroying all that wisdom ever prized,
Infecting every mob with all their hates.
I have a star for when the storm abates
A cock that crows against the coming day
England shall live like Pavilastukay."